Be a Frontline H.E.R.O!

A Parable to Propel Your Job & Life

Cyndi (Crother) Laurin, Ph.D.

Author of *Catch!* and *The Rudolph Factor*

Foreword

Think about your first jobs back when you were a teenager. They usually involved performing repetitive, mundane tasks and serving customers who barely noticed you...all for the privilege of working nights and weekends for minimum wage. It was a necessary rite of passage. How old were you when you dropped those jobs from your resume, if you ever included them at all?

Representing nearly *half* of the US workforce, hourly frontline employees are the backbone of the American economy. They are instrumental in breathing life into vital, "human" industries such as hospitality, retail and consumer services. Yet, these industries are plagued by low employee engagement which breeds high turnover and low customer satisfaction. Companies try to break this vicious cycle by addressing "culture", but only one individual has an outsized impact...the frontline manager.

Frontline supervisors and managers are often young. Remember when you were given keys and codes but few, if any, tools to deal with the complexities of managing your team? Learning the nuances of management can take many years. Unfortunately, they don't have that time because managers determine 70% of their employees' engagement. So ill-equipped, frontline managers unintentionally perpetuate the hire-train-repeat cycle for which there was no solution, no blueprint...until now.

Frontline teams are developing important skills that will inform their career paths and economic growth for years to come. That's why they deserve to be properly managed with tools designed specifically for *their* world and based on behavioral science. *Be a Frontline H.E.R.O.* provides a set of tools that give purpose and meaning to their work; tools that support their development while producing better outcomes for customers and companies alike.

I am certain you will enjoy *Be a Frontline H.E.R.O.* as part of a new way to manage a significant group of people on whom most of us depend. It's time to make work better.

Matt Robinson

Founder & CEO, Upfront

Acknowledgements

A special thank you to all of the reviewers who helped shape *Be a Frontline H.E.R.O* into its final iteration. It's always fun to experience how the manuscript evolves into something far better than the initial iteration. This is only possible with the various perspectives that provided me with valuable feedback. Thank you to my family, most notably, my mom, Cheryl Crother, who has faithfully reviewed each book I've written and my daughter, Emma, who always keeps me on my toes. Thank you to friends, Steve and Joanne Zdanko, for their thoughtful feedback as well.

Lastly, many thanks to the Upfront Works team, particularly Matt Robinson, who provided critical insights and feedback to improve the impact of the tools and story.

I also wish to express my gratitude to my Benedictine University Mesa, Training & Development Students who not only provided feedback for the book but also worked to create supportive training resources as well. Thank you George Adams, Bianca Alvarez, Tony Gomez, Brandon Barnes, Maria Campos Tello, Anthony DeRogatis, Nicolas Durazo, Omar Escobar Diaz, Ariah Evans, Gerves Fagan, Javon Fisher, Carson Frost, Garett Gahan, Jacob Gonzales, Bobby Henige, Adria Heriot, Anton Melendez, Sydney Nelson, Serena Nicolas, Savana Ramirez, Kelby Richardson, Jon Rivera, Lexi Tapia, and Trennon Udall. Many thanks to all again!

Table of Contents

Introduction: Falling into Frontline Management

I didn't know if I should feel excited or scared. I remember feeling both… and a little sick to my stomach. I couldn't believe I got promoted to shift manager. I'd only been working at Leo's Pizzeria for six months. While sad to admit, I had been there longer than anyone else aside from the cooks. I had never managed anyone before, but I was certain I would be better than the guy who was managing me. It was going to be nice to not be yelled at every day.

When I got the promotion, I thought, "*How hard can it be? All I have to do is make sure the orders are correct, people get their food quickly, and not screw things up! The food speaks for itself. We had great reviews online as long as you didn't read about our service.*" I had my fair share of managers since the time I started working. Some weren't too bad, but most had no idea what they were doing. Generally, I figured they would be gone in about three months. If anyone lasted longer than a few months as a shift manager, they were either really good or really bad. The really good ones ended up promoted to bigger and better jobs.

Before working at Leo's, I worked at a gym a few miles away. I had one great manager. She didn't last long because she got promoted to manage multiple locations. In the few months she was my boss, I watched and learned how she got things done. She was friendly but didn't let anything get by her. People respected her because she was consistent and fair, and she always let you know exactly where you stood. Despite her directness, you always knew she wanted you to be better. She was committed to us workers, and we did a lot to support the gym. After she left, though, the guy who replaced her was like a dictator. I think he was actually afraid of being a manager, so he just bullied people around the gym until they finally fired him.

With my new promotion and glass-half-full attitude, I believed I could make Leo's great. I suppose I was a little naïve. Okay, I was a lot naïve. Little did I know how hard it would be to manage a bunch of frontline workers, especially since I had recently been one myself and was replacing a horrible manager. Thank goodness I met Anne when I did. This is the story of how Anne changed my life in five days with five simple tools. Before I share about Anne, I should probably paint a picture of what working at Leo's was like before I met her.

It was my second week as shift manager at one of the Leo's Pizzeria locations. I didn't get any training because we were just too busy to fit it in. My boss, Tim, was the franchise owner. He was a good guy with good intentions, but he had multiple locations and was having a hard time keeping up with it all. He would pop in from time to time and to check and make sure everything was running smoothly. Tim had no idea what was going on when he wasn't here. It was pure chaos.

The other locations Tim owned were doing much better than ours. We were struggling. We had a decent amount of business because we were in a great location, but we could hardly keep people on staff. The turnover was crazy. Mike, the manager I replaced, had no management skills whatsoever. All he did was yell at people to get sh@# done. When that didn't work, he would just yell louder as if we couldn't hear him the first time. He would hang out in the back office most of the time. I had no idea what he was doing back there, but when he would come out, he just got in the way. God forbid someone called out. The rest of us would take the brunt of his anger. Sometimes, he would have to fill for no-shows. I hated those days. Mike never had anything nice to say. Even when we were really slammed and doing well, it was like it was just expected. He never once said, "Nice job!" Mostly, he would find something we did wrong and yell about it in front of everyone. It was awful. I couldn't imagine what he was like at his home. I felt sorry for his family. Under his rule, you had to have thick skin to work at Leo's.

Our bussers and servers would last about two months. Inevitably, basically everyone left within about three to four months of being hired. The pay wasn't great, but the building was clean and in a safer part of the city. The cooks seemed to last longer and were sort of immune to Mike's vengeance. I think they had an understanding. If the cook leaves, the business would be screwed. Mike wasn't a cook, so he treated them better than us up front. As much as I wanted to quit, I didn't. I thought about quitting every day. But let me be clear. I only stayed because the restaurant was a quick, five-minute bike ride from my house. It was in a nice location. I was good at my job and made fantastic tips. We were right downtown where all the action was. And, let's not forget the food. The food was great. People came from all over the city for our "Famous Leo's Pizza Pies." If they could just get the management piece right, it would have been an awesome place to work.

Mondays through Wednesdays weren't too bad, but Thursdays through Sundays were crazy busy. As a new manager, I was struggling to keep things afloat. Even after working with the bussers and waitresses on how things were supposed to go, they just didn't work together. They were super disrespectful to me. A few were just downright hateful to me. I wasn't sure if it was because I was now their manager after having recently been their coworker, or if they were just bad workers. I wanted to fire five of the fifteen employees I managed but was told I couldn't. Apparently, they had to do something "really bad" to fire them. It was hard to find new employees and even harder to keep them. If I was lucky enough to find a new server, they just didn't seem to care enough to make it matter. I knew it could be better, but I just didn't know how. I tried to be nice, then I tried to be mean, then I tried to help on the floor, then I tried just managing from the back office. I didn't know what the heck I was doing, and it showed.

Enter Anne. I'll never forget meeting her. She came in late on a Thursday night. I was pretty stressed out and had had it with the employees. The hostess called out sick, so I had to fill in for her. There was a huge conference going on just down the street, so we were twice as slammed as normal. Things were not going well. Servers were messing up orders; customers were sitting without drinks or appetizers and asking me for service. People were complaining to me about the service they were getting. And even worse, a faucet broke in the women's bathroom. I was at my wit's end and ready to throw in the towel. I had no more energy to try to make it work. I called the owner, Tim, for help. I rarely called him unless things were bad. He didn't answer his phone. I'm sure he knew if I was calling, things were indeed bad. When I finally did hear from him, he said he couldn't help. He wasn't available because he was dealing with a crisis at another location. I was on my own with no help, no plan, no tools, no nothin'.

"Hi! Welcome to Leo's. How many?" I was hardly able to force a smile at this point. All I could think about was the mess in the bathroom waiting for me to clean up and knowing that managing all this chaos was up to me. I felt like the proverbial chicken with its head cut off. I was running around in circles because I had too many issues and no tools to fix them.

"Just one," she said.

"Name?"

"Anne."

"Okay, Anne." I was writing her name on the long list of customers before her. "It's going to be quite a wait unless you don't mind sitting at the bar. There is one seat available in there. Is that okay?" She still had her name tag on from the nearby conference she was attending and looked like a nice person. Oddly, amidst the chaos, she looked like a peaceful person. I know it sounds strange, but there was something interesting about her.

Anne nodded and said, "Yes, the bar is fine. Thank you."

She followed me through the craziness to the bar, and said, "Boy, you guys are busy tonight."

I tried holding back my frustrations, but I couldn't help myself. "Yeah, I'll be glad when this night is over. Everything is falling apart, and this is only my second week as shift manager. I thought I could do this, but clearly, I'm in way over my head. It might have helped if I had been given a little training aside from sexual harassment training and how to run the cash register." I started laughing out of fear of starting to cry.

Anne laughed with me, but I'm sure she could tell I was a mess. "I know, right? I've been in your shoes before as well. It's been many years, but I know how you feel."

I thought to myself, *"Lady, you may think you know how I feel. I'm telling you, 'you have no idea what's happening here. I am quitting tonight as soon as my shift is over…..if I make it to the end of my shift. I'm done with this place!'"* Of course, on the outside I was forcing as genuine a smile I could muster.

"What can I get you to drink? Any appetizers to get started for you?"

Anne thought for a moment, checked the menu quickly, and said, "I'll take an iced tea with lemon and the sample platter appetizer. That'll be it for me."

"You got it." I turned to head back to the beverage station and noticed the tables were beginning to clear out a bit. The wave of customers was starting to subside. I started to take a deep breath, and then I remembered I needed to finish cleaning up the leaky faucet in the bathroom. I hollered to Rae to get the iced tea for Anne and found a busser sitting out back smoking. I told him to close the women's bathroom and finish cleaning it for me. I had complaining customers and other fires to put out, but things were finally beginning to slow down. I was exhausted and had a pounding headache.

As I looked around at the restaurant, I just shook my head. I'm too young to be feeling this stressed out for the little pay I make. I decided I would for sure quit after my shift. Sure, my pay increased a bit as shift manager, but it wasn't worth the stress and headache. Not only was I not getting tips anymore, the increase in pay was not enough to justify the amount of work I was doing. I had one great server, Rae, who I worked really well with. Unfortunately, there was only one Rae. I just couldn't do this for one more night. I knew the weekend coming was simply going to be a repeat of tonight. With the conference in town and no help, I would rather spend the time looking for a new job. I wanted to learn how to manage people, but this was not going to be the place to learn it.

The cook rang the bell for Anne's appetizer, so I grabbed it and headed her way. "Here you go. Is there anything else I can get for you?" I was exhausted, and it showed. Anne smiled at me empathetically and said, "How are you?" I shook my head and said, "Not good. I'm pretty much done with this. I can't do this anymore. I'm going to quit tonight and find another gig. It's upsetting because I'm not a quitter-type person. I thought I could do this, but I just have no support, no tools, nothing to help me with the exception of my best waitress, Rae. And even she isn't always here. It's just too much."

Anne listened, nodding her head and asked what time we closed. I told her we'd be closing at 2am, and we'd open again at noon the next day. She asked me my name, and I told her it was Emily. She said, "Emily, if you had five tools to catapult you into effectively managing Leo's, would you be interested?"

"Yes, but you sound like an infomercial. Sorry, but it sounds too easy – too good to be true. You know what they say about things that sound too good to be true..." I raised my eyebrow and gave her a funny face in disbelief.

Anne laughed and said, "Yes, I know what they say. I'm presenting at the conference tomorrow afternoon but have the morning available. If you are willing to learn some simple tools that will make an immediate difference, meet me here at Leo's tomorrow at 11:00am. Does that sound like something you'd be interested in?"

"Seriously? What's the catch?" I was waiting for Anne to say, "*It'll only cost you $199...but you can make ten payments of ...*" Okay, my head was feeling a little crazy. I looked at her straight in the eyes to see if I could detect any spec of deceit and said, "I'm exhausted but intrigued."

"No catch." The barstool next to Anne was available, and she asked me to sit for a minute. "Listen, Emily, I've been in your shoes. I remember wishing back then that I had someone to teach me how to manage others. I was a good worker, and I worked hard for very little money. When I was 18, I worked at a fancy hotel and was promoted to housekeeping manager after having only worked there for a couple of months. There was no training. I knew I didn't want to be a housekeeper forever. It was just a way to pass the time until I could figure out what I wanted to do. The potential for me to grow and make better money was there. So, I took the opportunity and struggled a lot for the first few months."

Anne continued, "Then I started trying out different things my friends shared. For example, one of my friends had a great manager, so I asked her to tell me what made her manager so great. Everything she shared, I tried. When I spent more time with my team, I started to learn some tools worked better than others. I developed my own tools as well. It wasn't very long before word got around, and people were asking if they could work for me. Believe me, it wasn't a quick process, nor was it an easy process. I made a ton of mistakes along the way. There were times I wanted to quit, but I was encouraged by the change I saw in myself and in the people around me."

I could see that Anne was genuinely empathetic to my situation. She went on to say, "In time, my manager recognized my growth and promoted me to a training position. I was responsible for training all of our frontline supervisors in our hotel chain cross the United States. Now, I teach the same five tools to franchise owners and small business owners in the retail, restaurant and hospitality industries. It is also what I'm presenting at the Conference down the street. If you are interested, consider it my way of paying it forward."

"Are you kidding? Wow, thank you! Okay, so I won't quit tonight. I will give this a chance. I'll meet you here at 11:00AM tomorrow." It almost felt surreal. I've always known sometimes the best things come out of the worst times of distress. This was clearly one of those times. I left Anne to finish her meal and jumped back into putting out fires and closing up for the night.

I woke the next day feeling anxious about meeting Anne. Last night had been such a mess. I started to doubt whether meeting Anne had actually happened. I didn't ask if I needed to bring anything or prepare in any way. I hadn't let my boss, Tim, know I was meeting with her and wasn't sure if I was even supposed to. All I knew was I couldn't do one more day at Leo's Pizzeria as it was. If Anne could help me, I might consider staying in the game for another day.

I hopped on my bike and headed over to Leo's at 10:30AM. It seemed to take forever for 11:00 to roll around. The morning crew was already prepping for the afternoon, and the morning shift manager, Mark, was in the back office. I let him know I was meeting a lady named Anne in a bit, and she was going to teach me some tools about management. Mark rolled his eyes, laughed at me, and wished me good luck. He said if I actually learned anything to tell him about it, but clearly he wasn't interested.

Mark was an older guy who had managed at some of Tim's other locations. He was a decent guy. He didn't offer to help me at all when I asked. He just told me I'd figure it out. I wish I had figured it out, but I didn't even know what I was supposed to be trying to figure out. I just didn't know what I didn't know, and apparently Mark wasn't going to tell me.

Anne arrived a little early, and I realized I was way more nervous about this than I thought I would be. My heart was pounding, and I felt a little dizzy like I was going to give a speech or something. "Hi, Emily!" Anne was dressed in jeans and quite a bit less formal than she was last night. She shook my hand. She had a firm handshake. My dad always told me to shake hands like you meant it. I told her how much I appreciated her taking time to help me.

We talked about the struggles of being a frontline manager and how disconnected the owner is from what's happening on the floor. I was brutally honest with her and told her I probably shouldn't even be a shift manager. I told her I had no idea what I was doing and tended to end up being a floating server throughout my shift because that's what I knew. It clearly wasn't working because I always felt like we were falling apart at the seams.

I told her how people would act all busy and productive when Tim showed up to check things out. Otherwise, I had to chase down workers who'd go outside to smoke or just leave without telling me. I had asked Tim what I should do to get people to work, and he laughed at me. Then, he told me to incentivize the workers. I asked if we could get some small gift cards, and he told me to not just give them out but make the servers compete for them. I tried to motivate them with the gift cards for about a week, but it didn't work at all. All I did was upset everyone who didn't get the gift card. I couldn't give them extra money or time off. Those seemed to be the only things wanted. When employees were late, all I could do was tell them to be on time. There are only so many times you can tell an employee to 1) show up, and 2) be on time. I was frustrated and felt like I was babysitting a bunch of kids.

I also shared how the communication was bad in the restaurant. We never knew what ingredients were coming in or what the specials would be until fifteen minutes before the shift started. So in a nutshell, I had been put in charge of managing our restaurant, but there was no way to manage the employees. It seemed like the only thing I could do was to give a gift card or shake my finger at them. I just bounced around the restaurant filling in for no-shows, telling people what to do, and hardly had enough time to actually get the numbers for Tim. Tim was frustrated with me that I wasn't managing to the numbers. When I told him I needed help because I didn't have time to get the numbers he wanted, he didn't understand. I told him I hardly had any time to do anything. He just kept telling me to delegate to others and to do a better job managing. As he liked to tell me, "*You* are the manager."

Anne listened, and I could tell from her reactions, she knew exactly where I was coming from. She wasn't surprised at anything I had shared. She nodded in agreeance, and I felt like she really did get it. And, I knew it wasn't just me. I'd worked at a lot of places in retail and hospitality, and believe me when I say no one – okay, let's be fair and say very, very few know how to manage effectively at the frontline level.

I went on to share, "Even worse, from my vantage point, I don't even think the owners or top managers know how to manage because clearly they're not managing down the line. They're totally disconnected. It feels like all they care about is profits, profits, profits. I get it. The company needs to make money to stay in business. But I gotta say, it's not exactly inspiring when *my* paycheck doesn't change whether we make more profits or not. What's important to them, and what's important to us on the frontline is completely different."

Anne stopped me. "I hear you. I believe you. I get it. You're absolutely right. You're not alone. Take a deep breath. There are millions of frontline shift managers and supervisors literally thrown into their role with no training aside from how to use the P.O.S. system or how to process goods or services. Some will get some customer service training which generally translates to, *'do whatever it takes to keep the customer from putting a bad review on social media.'* You're also correct by noticing the difference between what is important to the top line managers being quite different than the frontline. Know it's okay. We're not going to change the differing perspectives today. The tools I am going to share with you will create incremental improvements at your level, resulting in improving what is important to owners and higher level managers. They're going to be focused on profitability and revenues because they have to be. They have to have laser focus on the numbers, especially when they have multiple locations. Since I'm only in town for the next five days, what we want to accomplish here is giving *you* the tools *you* need to effectively manage *your team* on a day-to-day basis. As a natural result of your new and improved good management skills, the business will have greater profits. This doesn't have to be either/or. All levels of management can win what's important to them with these five simple tools I'm going to share with you. Not only that, Emily, but the skills you learn from these simple tools are highly sought after by all employers."

At this point, I was feeling optimistic but a little apprehensive. I asked Anne, "Five simple tools? Could it actually be that easy? And, if it is so easy, why don't we all have these tools in use already?" Anne reminded me of how I was promoted. It's the ol', *last one standing becomes the manager* routine. Anne explained that while the tools are not hard to understand, they require a commitment. She went on to share that while the frontline is the touchpoint between customer and goods/services, upper level managers and executives recognize turnover as a given. In other words, excessive levels of turnover are par for the course in the larger retail, food and hospitality industries. Even small, family-owned businesses expect a high level of turnover. Because it is expected, general thinking is there is no point in investing in training frontline supervisors or managers to actually manage because they will simply take the training to their next employer. Anne continued, "Training you is considered a cost, not an investment. Why pay for training you, when the statistics say you're going to leave Leo's Pizzeria in about three months? Make sense? Hence, the cycle continues."

Anne went on to say, "I'm devoting this phase of my career to working with those same companies and training frontline supervision and management at a *cost* they can't refuse. Like everything else in my life, this is an experiment. I have already seen significant improvement from frontline supervisors and managers who have committed to implementing these five tools, so without further ado, let's get started!"

"Emily, this is going to require a commitment from you as much as it is from me. I am in town for four more days for this conference. If you'll agree to meet with me for one hour before work for these next four days, I will share one tool per day with you, starting with the first tool right now. For this to be successful, you will need to actually use the tool learned for your shift."

I must have looked a little confused because Anne said, "Why, you ask? Research tells us we will forget seventy percent of what we've been taught if we don't use it within 24 hours. So, how this is going to work is I'll teach you a new tool before your shift to use during that shift, and I'll come the following day at 11:00am to see how it worked. After your shift, you should text me how it went while the events are still fresh in your mind. I want you to share what worked, what didn't, and what scenarios presented themselves that stumped you. I will coach you to make sure you are comfortable with each tool. Generally, I would recommend you experiment with each tool for at least one week before learning the next. However, because I'm just here for the next few days, let's work together to get you set up, and then we'll follow up via text or phone after I head back to Phoenix. Does that sound good to you?"

"Yes. Anne, I can't thank you enough for taking the time to help me learn how to manage. I seriously had planned on quitting last night. But, you've given me some hope. I'm going to give this a shot. My mom always tells to me to not quit something until I've given it my all, and I felt like I'd given every ounce of energy to no avail. But meeting you has changed things. I'll give the tools a try, and we'll see how it goes from there. It's the best I can do."

Anne responded, "Your mom was right. And you did give your all with your energy. Now, we are going to address management from a different approach. The hitch with energy is it's limited. You know that's true based upon how you felt last night. You were exhausted. And as I can attest to, your energy decreases as you get older!" Anne laughed. "Rather than focus on expending more energy to manage your team, we're going to use tools to change your *approach* to managing your team. This will allow you to know which tool to pull out of your tool belt depending on whatever situation arises. You'll kind of be a like a superhero!"

"Will your tools fix a leaky faucet in the women's bathroom?" We both laughed.

"No, that's called a wrench." Anne and I laughed some more and then got back to the business of learning how to be a frontline hero.

Anne continued, "We're going to consider these five tools as your 'frontline hero starter kit'. You need to know there are many more tools than the first five I'm going to share with you over the next few days. In time, as you learn more tools or develop your own, you can simply put them in your management tool belt."

I nodded my head, "A tool belt? Sounds good to me. What is tool number one?"

TOOL 1: The HUDDLE

Anne told me to take notes, so I grabbed a piece of paper and pen from the back office and was ready to go. "*The Huddle* is our first tool. It is a very simple tool to help you develop daily shared goals and objectives for your team. Often times, frontline employees have no idea about what they are supposed to do. They usually don't know much about the products or services they sell. They don't know why some things go on sale and others don't. Most workers are simply there to give the customer what the customer says they want. For example, if Leo's Pizzeria was to offer a special or a promotion, you had mentioned no one knows what it was going to be until it gets written on the front board for the customers to see. However, the servers may not even know about it unless they happen to go read the board as well. Another example might be a hair salon wants to upsell a particular product during a promotion, but the staff may or may not be aware of what the product is, if it's any good, how to use it, how long the promotion is running, and even worse, what the goals are...other than sell as much as possible. There may be incentives to push product, but there isn't a standard form of communicating about what needs attention from day to day. This is your responsibility as the frontline shift manager or supervisor."

Anne continued, "The Huddle is a tool used to effectively start and finish each shift. Write this part down. 'It should take 5 – 10 minutes.' That's it. Emily, the Huddle gives you an opportunity to align your team to daily short-term objectives. For example, you could use the Huddle to drive one of Leo's specials. Or, if you want to create a customer service initiative, you could use the Huddle to let the team know today's objective is for every employee to make eye contact and smile to each customer. It could be a product-based, where you let the team know the goal for the day is to sell twenty jars of Leo's Famous Pizza Sauce. Regardless of what the day's initiative is, the Huddle gives you a way to communicate the most important things to focus on for any specific shift."

Anne was right. This sounded like an easy tool to use, and I could already see how this would help my team get on the same page. "Anne, you mentioned something about doing the Huddle at the end of the shift as well? How does that work?"

Anne nodded and said, "Yes, especially in fast-paced environments like Leo's Pizzeria or a retail store, having an end-of-day Huddle will give your team a brief opportunity to talk about how they did. If something unexpected came up, this provides an opportunity for everyone to learn from it. If we waited until the next day, often times we've already forgotten about it and are likely to continue making the same mistakes. It also works in conjunction with the other tools, but we'll get to those in the coming days."

It sounded so easy. I felt dumb asking, but I wasn't sure how to actually use the tool "Okay, Anne, it sounds simple enough. So, how exactly does the Huddle go? How do I start it? What am I supposed to say? Can you walk me through how to do the Huddle?"

"Of course!" Anne clapped her hands together and continued, "So, today at noon when your team comes in, tell them you have some announcements to make. They all, and I mean ALL, must come up to the front of the restaurant. This includes the back – cooks and all – as well as the front staff. Tell them to circle close so everyone can hear and see each other." I was writing this down as fast as I could. Anne sort of tapped on the table and said, "If someone sits down, just tell them it is a super quick meeting so everyone should be standing unless they have a physical reason they cannot stand. Watch their body language as they might be nervous or resistant about what's happening. It could very likely be the first time they will have participated in a Huddle. You'll need to do a little extra explaining the first time."

"Okay, so far so good," I looked up at Anne for the next step.

"Then, during the Huddle, make good eye contact with each person on your team, telling them you are going to start and end each shift doing a brief *standing* Huddle to help get and keep everyone on the same page. It's important everyone is standing to encourage the speediness of the event. You can start by saying, '*Thanks for joining me for a minute. I realize things aren't running terribly smoothly, and I'm working to make Leo's a place we can all enjoy. Starting today, we're going to do a brief Huddle at the start of our shift (just like football teams do a huddle before each play). It's going to take about 5 – 10 minutes, and the purpose is to give me an opportunity to get us on the same page. The Huddle will likely be a little different each day. I'm going to share our daily specials, promotions we're running, or any other news we all need to know. And, I'm going to ask if there is anything in the way of accomplishing our goal or objective for the day. Does it make sense to everyone? Does anyone have any questions for me? At the end of the shift, we're going to get back together for another 5 – 10 minutes to check in on how the shift went. I learned from a friend who uses Huddles regularly that this is a significant factor in the success in the World Famous Pike Place Fish Market in Seattle. You know the place where they holler and throw the fish. We're going to give it a go here at Leo's as well. Sound good? Great! We've just completed our first huddle.'*"

"That's it?" I asked. "It seems too easy. What am I missing?"

Anne said, "It's not about the complexity of the topic. It's about creating and committing to a standard process every day when the shift begins and ends with regular but brief communication. After a while, it becomes a habit that everyone expects here at Leo's. As you and your team become more comfortable with the Huddle, we can talk about delegating who runs the Huddle to different members of your team. It'll take a little while to get there, but shared leadership is the ultimate goal we're seeking with the Huddle. And you're right. It is a simple tool in theory, but it takes some time and repetition for it to become part of the culture. Don't give up if members of your team are resistant. You have to remember they haven't been given much attention in the past, and you're investing time with them. This new attention can create some discomfort at first. Work through any resistance, and keep a brief journal of how it's going so when we follow up with each other, I can coach you through specific incidents that may occur. For the most part, it's been my experience that teams like being on the same page. They like being pointed in a direction, even if it's just to promote a special or small initiative. People like feeling like they're part of a winning team. It doesn't happen by itself. The shift manager has the ability to make it happen. In the longer run, the daily Huddles set the foundation for larger initiatives requiring the team to be lock-step on the same page. Does this make sense?"

"Yes, it makes perfect sense. And I love that it's quick, to the point, and becomes a part of the culture here. Looks like it's time for me to get to work. Wish me luck. I've got a Huddle to run!" I pushed back my chair to get up and felt excited and nervous all at the same time.

"Excellent!" Anne stood up, and we shook hands. As she left to prepare for her presentation, I checked my notes again to prepare for our first Huddle at Leo's:

1. 5 – 10 minutes

2. Everyone standing

3. Keep it simple

4. Share "Action of the Day":

    a. Daily Special

    b. Promotion

    c. Product to Sell

    d. Customer Service Practice

I took a deep breath as my staff started showing up for our shift.

"Hey guys. Can you all come up front for a quick announcement?" I was a lot more nervous than I thought I was going to be. I could feel my heart pounding through my shirt.

"Are you quitting?" Rae put her hands up to her mouth and then covered her eyes.

"No, not today." I laughed but realized less than twelve hours ago, quitting *had* been my plan. "So, I get last night was a bust, and I didn't do a great job of managing everything. I want to make this a place you guys like working, and I'm trying out some new ways to help us. A friend of mine told me about doing Huddles at her work. You know, like what football teams do before each play. The idea is to get us all on the same page. So, this is it! We're having our first one right now! They're going to be really quick. I am planning just five to ten minutes, and we're going to do them at the beginning and end of each shift."

"The end of each shift?" said Gerry, one of my best cooks. I have to leave as soon as we're done because I have to get home to my family. I live 45 minutes away." Gerry looked visibly upset about having to stay. I had to think on my feet quickly because I was afraid I'd start losing them if one person got upset.

"No, don't worry, Gerry. We're not staying after work. This won't add any additional time to the night. We're going to start closing procedures ten minutes earlier than we normally do. We'll have a quick huddle to recap how everything went. Listen, this is going to be helpful in getting us working better as a team. I can see a lot of value in it, and I hope you can see the value, too."

"I think it's a great idea!" Rae raised her hand as if she was in school. "There are so many times I have no idea what the specials are, or the customer is ordering something I've never heard of. I have to run up to the front to see what they heck they're talking about. I think it's great to get us on the same page. I think it'll help a lot. I'm game."

Whew. It was helpful to have Rae agree. Everyone liked Rae, so having her stamp of approval with the Huddle went a long way. I thought about it more and thought I might share the new tools I was learning with Rae so she could continue to be an advocate to get the other employees on board. Ten minutes felt like thirty seconds, and then we got to work.

When we were done with our first Huddle, Chad, one of my new bussers, said, "Go team!" Everyone laughed, and for the first time, I was hopeful the tools Anne was sharing with me were actually going to make a difference.

After our shift, well…ten minutes before the end of our shift, I managed to wrangle the team back for our end-of-shift Huddle. While there a little eye rolling initially, I kept it simple. I made sure everyone was standing. I told them I appreciated their playing along in doing the Huddles with me. I broke into a dance move pretending to be doing the

Hustle, but the joke didn't go over too well. I could see they were apprehensive but willing to give it a try. Quite frankly, at this point, their willingness was the best I could ask for.

I biked home after we closed and texted Anne to give her the details of how the Huddle went. I thanked her again for everything and looked forward to learning about the second tool.

Right on schedule, Anne met me at Leo's at 11:00AM sharp. We were both smiling in anticipation of talking about how the Huddles went. We sat down to get started. I had my paper and pen in hand today, and she said, "So, it sounds like it went well. You had a bit of resistance from the cook, but it sounds like you came up with a good solution on the spot. Sounds like a success. How did it feel   from your perspective?"

"I felt pretty good about it. You know, it's funny. It is a simple tool to talk about and learn about. It was even easy to walk through with the team. However, the not-so-easy part was how to manage what comes up, like the concern about staying after hours. What if I can't think of a solution, or worse, if the solution I propose isn't actually feasible? I'm a little worried I'm setting myself up to fail. How do I know how to respond to everything?" I looked to Anne for some reassurance.

"Well, that's a good point to talk about. Remember the goal of the Huddle isn't to solve or resolve everything that comes up during the Huddle. The goal is to get everyone aligned to the same daily objective. That's it. As you find any resistance or issues come up, those becomes your 'Manager To-Do List' to resolve outside, or after, the Huddle. The problem a lot of young managers have is they think they have to react to, or solve, every problem comes up at every moment. We both know fixing every issue at the moment it is discovered would set up any manager to fail at some point. So, add in your notes that the intention is to simply get the team on the same page. Write this down. We want to *align behaviors to a daily goal or objective.* Sometimes, these will come from the owner of Leo's. Didn't you say his name is Tim?"

"Yes, the owner's name is Tim. He's a good guy." I felt like I needed Anne to know that Tim has good intentions, despite his not having time to train me.

"That's good," Anne went on to say, "Other times, the daily goal or objective will be something you have personally observed or want to focus on. In any case, they should be what are known as 'SMART' goals, meaning they are **s**pecific, **m**easurable, **a**chievable, **r**elevant, and timely each day. Does this make sense?"

I felt a sense of relief and said, "Yes, it makes a lot of sense. I was thinking I had to fix whatever came up in the Huddle. But now I understand to use the Huddle to align our team to the *play of the day*, like we're a football team. Okay, so now what?"

Anne pulled a 5" x 7" card out of her briefcase for me to hang in the back office to remind me of the purpose and how to do the Huddle. It showed the steps I would follow to ensure it was a success. She congratulated me for a job well done, and I couldn't wait to learn about tool two. I felt good and knew I was on the right track. If the other four tools were as easy as this, I began to think it might actually be possible to make Leo's a great place to work.

TOOL 2: The POSITION TO NOTICE

I didn't have much to offer Anne in return for her time and tools, but I knew she was here for the conference and was probably missing lunch to take time to meet with me. I asked her if she wanted something to eat, and she smiled and said, "No, thank you for asking. I will take a glass of iced tea, but I will be back for dinner tonight. I'll have to try something different on Leo's menu." I got up and got us both some iced tea, and we started to talk about tool two.

"Ok, Emily, let's talk about tool two. I call it *The Position to Notice*." Anne pulled another card out of her briefcase, similar to the first, to hang in the back office. She went on to share, "The 'Position to Notice' is also known as the 'Walkabout' and helps the manager maintain a pulse on how the day's goals and objectives are going to ensure the business is on track. So, yesterday you learned how to use the Huddle to kick off and end the shift. You were successful in having your first Huddles, and now you're ready to be in a Position to Notice. Being in a Position to Notice ensures the team is doing things during the shift to support the daily goal. It's an easy way to keep the train on the tracks. Aligned with the Huddle, the Position to Notice should be happening throughout the day."

"So I just walk around the restaurant?" I was a little miffed at the simplicity of this tool as well.

"Basically, yes. You should be out on the floor nearly your full shift. The exception for being in the back office is for conducting payroll or sending data to Tim.

Obviously, when you are in the back office, you can't be in a Position to Notice if your team is doing things to stay on track or doing things that need to be adjusted a bit. Rather than meandering around, however, a Position to Notice is an activity with the purpose of *intentional observation*. The challenge in this tool is observing whether the activities and tasks your team is doing are supporting the daily goal or objective that you shared in the start-of-shift Huddle. Or, you may observe actions or behaviors are not aligned to the daily goal and need some adjusting. So, let's get into a Position to Notice at Leo's." We both laughed and got up from our chairs to practice.

"Most frontline managers I've worked with tend to spend a lot of time doing one of two things not related to *managing* the frontline. They tend to either perform the work that should be done by their employees. In which case, this tool could be called 'the resist the urge to take over' tool. Or, they are in the back office where they're unable to see or hear what they should be managing on the floor." Anne and I headed back to the back office so she could see where it was and what it looked like. I told her how my last manager, Mike, would sit in the office for most of the day and then come out and yell at us when we were doing something wrong.

Anne said, "Sounds like Mike didn't have any tools in his tool belt except for a carrot and a stick." I must have looked confused because Anne looked back at me a little puzzled and said, "What I mean is it sounds like he would either reward or punish, which is more like parenting, not managing."

"Yes, he was missing a tool belt. But he didn't use the carrot. Only the stick. Well, actually he would try to give us incentives to work harder, which would usually turn into pitting us against each other. I guess that was the carrot. But mostly, he just told us what to do." I shuddered a bit just thinking about thosedays.

Anne shared more, "As you become better at the Position to Notice, you will eventually be able to understand what your employees need from you. You'll be able to see what they're good at, what challenges them, and have a pretty accurate pulse on how they are doing. You will be able to comfortably advise them on standard processes. You will gain knowledge about how work is performed and likely find opportunities to improve your team's overall performance. However, much like the Huddle, in the early days, Emily, you will want to keep it simple. When it comes to managing the frontline, simple is best. Many managers tend to overcomplicate things. These tools are intended to keep it simple."

"What does 'simple' look like?" I felt stupid asking the question, but I had no idea what I was supposed to be looking for.

"Great question!" Anne told me to act as though I was a server and clean tables but to also watch her move about. There were no customers in the restaurant because we would be opening at noon. She went back to the back office area and came out as if she was the shift manager on duty. She first walked back through the kitchen area and said hello to the staff in back. Then, she came out front and looked throughout the restaurant as if she was making sure everything was in place. She made her way around the tables and then came up to me. "Hey, Emily, how is everything going tonight?"

"Going good," I said. I wasn't sure if I was supposed to make something up, so I just stuck to simple.

Anne persisted a bit more, "I see you're doing a great job cleaning the tables. That helps us turn the tables quickly. Keep it up! I really appreciate you and your hard work." Then she motioned me to come sit back down. We headed back to our table, and I was surprised at how quick and straightforward the process was. "So, you see, Emily, with the Position to Notice, you're truly just intentionally checking the environment out. Is everything in its place? Are the employees looking focused or like they need something? Being in a Position to Notice allowed me to see that you were doing something that helps the company, so I let you know."

"Cleaning tables?" I was perplexed, "Isn't that just expected as part of my job?"

"Yes, Emily! This brings up an excellent learning point. The Position to Notice should allow you to recognize the simple, yet important things individuals are doing on a daily basis. I'm getting a little ahead of myself with the next tool, but it allowed me the opportunity to tell you to, 'Keep It Up'. Generally, frontline workers only hear from their manager when they're doing something wrong. The Position to Notice should have you also looking for what employees are doing right."

"I've never thought of that before. I've never thought of telling employees they are doing well when they are just doing their job, but it did make me feel good when you told me that you appreciated how well I was cleaning the table. I can see how this will make my team feel as well." I was genuinely surprised at how that one played out.

Anne continued, "Now, recognize you're not to become the gopher to go get stuff they can generally get for themselves. You're not checking if they need help to do their jobs. Don't allow yourself to get sucked into doing their work for them. Remember, you are the manager. You're there to provide support and recommendations so they can do their jobs more effectively. Make sense? To be in a Position to Notice you have to be committed to resisting the urge to take over."

"Yeah, I think I can do it. So, on tonight's frontline management menu, I now have one Huddle, followed by being in a Position to Notice things my team is on track, and wrapping up with an end-of-shift Huddle. What do I do when I notice we're on track...or off track?"

Anne smiled, raised her hands into the air and clapped, "Excellent work! You've identified our next two tools! For tonight, I just want you to focus on being in a Position to Notice and letting your team know when you are observing tasks they are doing that are helpful to the restaurant – even if they are tasks that are expected to be done. Be in a position to observe specific desired behaviors that help Leo's and to observe undesired behaviors that need to be adjusted. I'll be back for dinner around 9:00pm, so please let me know how it's going if time allows. Even a quick thumbs up or down my way will tell me how you are doing. As with last night, write down anything you observed, anything you felt was working, wasn't working, or anything you want to discuss when we talk about it again tomorrow." With that, Anne packed up her things and headed back to the conference center.

My employees starting coming in to start our shift, and they must have noticed I was feeling pretty good or better about things because they, too, seemed more chipper than normal. Even though I wasn't quite as confident on the inside as I was looking on the outside, I didn't skip a beat and called the team over for our second kick-off Huddle.

"Hey guys, so for this Huddle, the plan for tonight is for the front to promote the Linguine con Vongole (Linguine with clam sauce). The clams are one of those highly perishable items that don't last long, so I'd love to see us sell out of this meal. We have enough ingredients to sell 75 plates. For the back, I'll be coming around regularly to check in and see how we're doing. Let's keep track of how many plates we serve with a simply tally mark on the white board in back, and I'll make sure the front is aware as well. Is there anything I can help with after we're done here?" Everyone just listened and looked at me. Nobody said anything, and

I thought for a second to ask more questions, but I pictured Anne saying to keep it simple. "No? Okay then, let's sell 75 Linguini con Vongole!"

Wow, I felt great! For the first time, I felt like I was *managing* the team. They were listening and seemed interested in what I was saying.

Same busser as yesterday, Chad, said, "34 – 67 – 14 – huh – huh – hike!" Everyone laughed again, and I was feeling like we were starting to find our way to working together. It was a good feeling.

It was Friday night, and with the larger-than-normal conference crowd, things started to derail a bit after a couple of hours. I remembered Anne said to be in a Position to Notice desired and undesired behaviors, but I'd been so busy, I had totally forgotten to do it. I made a quick note to remind myself to talk to Anne about when to observe and when to jump in. Then, I went back to the back office, looked at the card on the wall and said to myself, "Keep the Position to Notice simple, Emily. Ok, today's goal was 75 linguine with clam sauce. Go check the board and let the hostess and servers know. Keep it simple. Keep it simple."

I left the office with Anne's demonstration in my head. I went back into the kitchen and asked how we were doing with the linguine and clam sauce. The head cook said, "We're looking good. We've delivered 42 to the servers." I nodded and gave him the thumbs up and left. Then I remembered I hadn't asked if they needed anything, so I went back and double checked. He looked sort of surprised when I came back in and said all was good. Then he gave me the thumbs up and smiled. I don't think I've ever seen that guy smile before. This is good. This is very good.

I went out into the main part of the restaurant. I checked in with the hostess to let her know we had 33 linguine with clam sauce specials left, asked a handful of customers if they were doing okay, and then was able to check in with the servers and bussers. I was able to let the servers know that we had 33 specials left to sell. For the first time, I actually sort of felt like this was *my* restaurant. It was surprising to me because I didn't expect to feel so strongly about it. Just a few days ago, I was going to quit, and with two tools under my belt (or in my belt), I was feeling pretty darn good. Still some chaos around me, but I was working through it.

Anne came in at 9:00pm as planned. I had a nice seat at the bar reserved for her. She could see we were moving fast and gave me a quick glance as if to ask, "How's it going?" I gave her a thumbs-up with a smile. After a large party of twelve people from the conference left, I was able to head over to her in the bar and tell her I'd completed the Huddle and did okay with my first Position to Notice. I shared the team seemed to be responding pretty well but that I was struggling a bit to find the time to be in a Position to Notice and had almost forgotten to be intentional about observing. Anne laughed and told me everything takes a little time to learn and asked me, "Is it better today than yesterday?"

"It sure is," I replied. Anne shook her head in acknowledgment and told me to focus on that. She continued, "As long as it's one percent better than yesterday, that's all that matters."

I was having some troubles with one of my servers, and her performance – or lack thereof – was causing me to jump in to assist more than I'd like. I shared with Anne how this was taking me away from checking in and managing the floor. I also realized I wasn't sure how much I needed to tell the workers they were doing well.

To my surprise, Anne said, "Perfect!" I gave her a puzzled look, and she laughed and said, "I have a tool for that! You'll learn all about it." We both laughed, and I left her to eat her dinner.

The night was extremely busy. It certainly provided ample random challenges, but at least I felt like I had a tiny bit of control of it. Like Anne said, at least more control than yesterday. We finished up the evening a little late, but we still did a closing Huddle. I let Gerry leave as scheduled to get to his family and quickly updated the others with the results of our linguine and clam sauce efforts. This Huddle wasn't even five minutes long, but I didn't want to skip it. I also wanted to keep to my commitment to not hold employees late for the Huddle. I realized this was a fine line to balance. It would have been all too easy to not do the closing Huddle, but I did it. I wanted to ask Anne about skipping things because I didn't know if it was okay or not. I sure had a lot to think about as I rode my bike home from work.

TOOL 3: The KEEP IT UP!

11:00AM came and went, and Anne was nowhere to be found. I started to worry a bit because the woman was literally like clockwork. I checked my phone but didn't see any messages from her, so I texted her a quick note to see if she was able to come in. Seconds after I clicked the *send* button, Anne came in looking a little distressed.

"What's up, Anne? Everything okay?" I took her briefcase and set it on a chair and then got her an iced tea from the bar.

"Thank you. Yes, everything's fine. I ended up get caught up with a franchise executive who wanted to learn more about the tools I am presenting at the conference. Big surprise, they are the same five tools I'm sharing with you! We got to talking, and the time sort of slipped away from me. It could be an amazing opportunity, and I'm sorry I didn't text or email you to let you know I was running a bit late."

"No problem. I was worried something might have happened. Do you think the franchise is going to hire you?" I could see Anne was excited just talking about it. She was passionate about her work, and I found her enthusiasm to be inspiring.

"It's looking pretty promising. The thing is, Emily, there are millions of frontline managers and supervisors all over the globe who, just like you, are struggling to retain and manage the performance of frontline employees. We both know they are a tough group to manage. Depending on what industry we're looking at, turnover of the frontline ranges from 30-90 percent. The fast-food industry tends to have the highest turnover of employees ranging between 150-400 percent! Restaurants, healthcare and hospitality turnover comes in a little lower. Retail and warehouse staff tend to turnover even less, but still more than what would be considered healthy."

"I didn't know there was such a thing as *healthy* turnover. What's considered healthy?" I realized I had no idea about turnover whatsoever, what was bad or good. I actually thought the goal was no turnover.

Anne said, "Great question! A healthy turnover – outside of frontline employment – would be 10-15 percent. The franchise exec I was talking to said their turnover was around 65 percent, which is pretty good for the fast-food industry. However, they have nearly 240,000 employees globally, so even moving the needle a few percentage points in retention can impact the customer experience in an incredibly meaningful way. Retention also creates millions of dollars of savings per year that could be invested back into employee growth and development. Frontline retention is *big* business. Ironically, businesses currently do very little in terms of retention efforts of frontline workers or managers."

"Wow, I had no idea. I'm so grateful to have met you, Anne. I'm learning so much so fast, and I'm already seeing immediate changes in myself and my team just with the first tools you've shared so far. Do we have time for the next tool today? What's tool three?" I was eager to get started because I knew we only had about 20 minutes before Leo's was open for lunch.

Anne nodded her head and said, "Yes, absolutely! Tool three won't take much time at all as it is directly related to what we talked about yesterday. We call it the 'Keep It Up'."

"The Keep It Up? Like keep doing it, keep it up?" I was confused.

"Yep, you got it, girl! Do you remember yesterday when we did our role play with you cleaning tables, and I told you that I appreciated your cleaning the tables and to Keep It Up?" Anne raised her eyebrows and nodded her head like she'd tricked me.

I laughed and said, "Oh, I get it. So, when you told me about being in a Position to spot the good things my employees were doing and to tell them, you were already talking about the Keep it Up!" It made sense, but much like the other tools, I was wondering if there was some catch to it, so I asked, "Okay, so why not just say, '*Nice job, Emily*!' and give me a thumbs up. Where does the tool part come in?"

"Good point!" Anne pulled out the fourth card and said, "Being told *'Nice job'* from the manager is nice, but often times, the worker doesn't know what part of what they were doing was being recognized. If the specific behavior isn't pointed out, the chances of the employee gaining awareness of what actions or behaviors to do again is quite low. Consider it being like throwing darts at a dartboard with a blindfold on. You don't see you hit the target, but the manager says, 'Great job, Emily!' With a blindfold, you're left to wonder or assume what your manager saw. Did you hit the board in general, or did you hit the bullseye?

"Oh, I got it. It makes total sense. That's actually happened to me in the past. I had a manager who would always tell people they were doing good work, but we'd get in trouble sometimes for what we thought was the same exact thing that had been complimented in the past." I rolled my eyes, and Anne laughed.

"The idea behind the Keep it Up is to recognize people doing the right thing, and there is specific language to use every time. The goal is to acknowledge observed, desired behaviors. The first and most important element is that you are *specific*."

Anne reached into her briefcase and pulled out another card for me to hang in the back office. She tapped on the card and said, "Okay, Emily, let's see you act this one out with me. You mentioned a couple of days ago you had a very supportive server. What was her name again?"

"Rae is her name. She's great. She's my best server. She's fast, friendly and very accurate with her orders. Customers request her table because she remembers their names, even if they've only come in a few times. I wish all of my servers were like Rae."

Anne shook her head and said, "Perfect! Let's do the Keep It Up on one specific behavior you want to ensure Rae is aware of so she can see the 'bullseye' of desired behaviors of a server. Are you ready?"

"Yes." I reviewed the card for a minute and thought about what specific behavior Rae did that I wanted her to keep doing. "Does it have to be only one?" Anne nodded yes to me, so I thought a bit more. Ah, I wanted her to keep being her friendly, smiley self with customers. "Okay, I'm ready. Here goes. Wait, should I do the Keep It Up on the floor with others around or in private?"

"Good thinking." Anne nodded her head like she was impressed with my question. "This should be done right on the floor. In fact, it's preferable if other employees hear because they, too, will learn what specific, desired behaviors get recognized. Okay, let's do it."

I checked the card one more time and said, "Hey Rae, I see you're so friendly and always smile to our customers, and you even remember their names. This has a great impact on the whole business because I see how much your customers appreciate it. Quite honestly, the whole team benefits from your friendliness." I felt stuck for a second and sputtered. "How do you do it, especially when it gets chaotic here?"

Anne smiled really big and said, "Oh, thanks, I guess I'm just a glass-half-full kind of person."

I kind of laughed and said, "Me, too! Well, keep it up, and know I appreciate you and your positivity." I knew I went a little off script and asked Anne if it was okay.

"Yes, of course! It's as important to recognize specific, desired actions and behaviors from our employees as it is to be yourself. The Keep it Up should sound like you! This is the true value of tool number two, the Position to Notice. When you observe effective activities, you immediately do the Keep It Up at the time it was observed. While the base language is very important, it's okay to add or modify a bit to feel more like you. However, you always want to start Keep It Up using specific, *observable* language like we talked about. '*I see…*' *or* '*I hear…*' We also can use '*I understand*…' because sometimes we have to address things we didn't actually see or hear but understand them to be true. If you didn't write this down in your notes already, remember to avoid saying, '*I feel…*' or '*I think*…' Does this all make sense?"

"Yes, this is an easy one. I love telling employees they're doing a great job, and I can see the value in being very specific about what I'm seeing that deserves praise. I like it, and I'm feeling like…or should I say, 'I understand' it will be easy for employees to receive as well. In the restaurant business, recognition goes a long way because you usually only get talked to when you're doing something wrong." I thought back to the relatively few times my managers had recognized specific things I was doing right.

Anne told me to pull out my notebook again and add some extra points in using the Keep It Up.

"First," she said, "It is vitally important that you provide balanced feedback to your employees. We are going to learn how to adjust undesired behavior tomorrow, but in the meantime, you should be aware of a three to one ratio on feedback. What I mean is that for every three times you recognize desired behaviors, you will likely adjust one undesired behavior. Balanced feedback means that you are committed to your employees being successful and doing well. This means that you will provide positive feedback and corrective. So, 3:1 Keep it Ups to Adjusts. We'll talk more about the corrective tool, the Adjust, tomorrow.

"Second, there needs to be consistency with providing feedback *every day* to your employees. These are not tools to be used only once in a while. All five tools, every day, and throughout the day.

"Third, your feedback has a 24-hour expiration. You must recognize or adjust observed behaviors within 24 hours of seeing or hearing them. The closer you can provide feedback to the action or behavior, the more impact it will have on your employee. Also, documenting feedback is important. The rule of thumb is if it isn't documented, it didn't happen. This is true for both positive and corrective feedback.

"Lastly, and we'll spend more time on this tomorrow with our next tool, but the Position to Notice and the Keep it Up are really one tool. The idea being, *'you see it, you recognize it...'*"

Anne asked if I wanted to practice one more Keep It Up, but we were getting short on time, and I had to get ready for our kick-off Huddle. I thanked her again, let her know I'd have her spot reserved for that evening, and wished her luck on the franchise opportunity she shared with me. She walked out of Leo's with a big smile on her face saying, "Keep it up!!!" I laughed. Anne had a good sense of humor.

TOOL 4: The ADJUST

Anne arrived at Leo's right on time. After I shared the opportunities where I was able to give specific Keep it Ups, we jumped right into discussion about the fourth tool. She asked me to tell her about the server I was having trouble with, so I told Anne her name was Jessica. She'd been with the restaurant for quite some time. I had heard she was related to the owner, Tim. She was maybe a niece or something. I didn't know for sure, but given the way she worked, it wouldn't have surprised me if she was a family member. She was slower than the other servers. She also tended to mess up customer orders a lot. She didn't act like she even cared to be there, and her actions showed it.

Anne asked me how I was *managing* her. I was embarrassed to admit I wasn't. I mean, I kept telling her the customers were waiting for her or needing this or that. I was regularly reminding her she'd forgotten something for customers and stepping in to assist, but that was it. I would just do things for her to keep the customers happy. One time, Jessica forgot to bring out a dish for a customer who was at a table with a party of eight people. I had noticed the guy was just sitting there and looked angry. When I asked if there was a problem with his meal, he said, "Yeah, I don't have one!"

So, I quickly took his order again and ran it to the kitchen and asked our cooks for a favor. We ended up taking the same order from another table that was ready to be delivered and giving it to Jessica's unhappy customer. He still wasn't happy. I apologized and offered to comp his meal. He seems to be okay with it. Jessica was nowhere to be found. I asked her what happened, and she said, "Oh, man, I totally forgot." I was so mad at her. I said, "Forgot? Are you kidding me? Did you not notice the man had no food in front of him? Everyone else at the table was nearly done!"

Jessica's response was, "Geez, he got his food, didn't he?" I couldn't believe my ears. I wanted to fire her on the spot. With all the mistakes and her poor attitude, there were plenty of reasons to fire her, but I wasn't allowed to. So, I just continued to do her work for her. At least I knew it would be done. It made me resent her. But as I spoke with Anne, I was beginning to see it was also my fault. I wasn't managing her performance at all. My resentment towards her was actually me being mad at myself for not managing her.

I shared all of this with Anne, and she said, "I get where you're coming from. And, you're right, you haven't been *managing* her." Even though I knew it was true, it was a little hard to hear out loud from this person I'd come to respect so much. Anne continued, "I totally understand why you have been filling in and making up for her poor performance. Also recognize when you do her work, you can't manage Leo's. You remove yourself from being in a Position to Notice, and then things can quickly get off track."

I couldn't agree more, but I didn't know what else to do. If I couldn't fire her, I definitely needed whatever tool four was so I could start managing her today. I told Anne I was ready for the next tool.

Anne began, "Tool four is called *The Adjust*. This one is also very easy to talk about and learn. Remember how easy it was to do the Keep it Up yesterday?"

I nodded and smiled, "I liked the Keep it Up! I'm going to keep up with the Keep it Up!" We both laughed.

Anne's face got a little more serious which made me pay attention. "The Adjust is the same exact idea. We measure progress step-by-step, not mile-by-mile when it comes to managing others. The Adjust is the same four-step process as the Keep it Up; however, in this case, we are level-setting, or adjusting another person's specific, *undesired* behavior. It can be a little tricky in practice because you are basically setting expectations you want to see or hear often times *after* seeing or hearing what you don't want. In the simplest of terms, the Adjust is used to establish or refine behavioral expectations. The beauty of it is that it gives guidance to your team to let them know specifically what is expected of them."

Anne continued, "For example, if the server is expected to bring drinks within two minutes of seating a customer, then bringing drinks within two minutes is the expectation. They can only perform to that expectation when they know what the expectation is. In this case, if the server is taking four minutes, you would have been in a Position to Notice and would have said, 'I see the customers at table five have not received their drinks. When it is delayed, it causes the customer to become frustrated and might delay getting meals ordered in a timely fashion. Help me understand why it took four minutes?' Then you would listen to the employee to hear for things that you can address. After they have shared their perspective, you can remind the employee about the two-minute drink expectation and ask them what they will do the next time a similar scenario presents itself."

Anne shared the research she had learned around correcting (or adjusting) behaviors. She said many managers are not effective because they do not address undesired behaviors right away, or worse, they do not address at all. When not addressed, the worker doesn't know, and the manager tends to start resenting that person assuming they should know already. It's not a good situation for anyone. Everyone needs to know what all of the different expectations and policies are when they are first hired and trained. If training isn't currently happening, it would be a good place to start. Often times, for whatever reason, employees do not perform the task as expected, and then negative consequences happen. The customer is upset, gives a bad review online, or whatnot.

Anne went on to say, "In conjunction with the Position to Notice, the Adjust is a tool to help the manager identify a specific, unwanted behavior and very effectively let the employee know in real time what the desired expectation is moving forward. Sometimes, just making the employee aware of what is expected is enough to change the behavior. Other times, it takes a series of incidents to change the behavior. And, even still, sometimes the end result is terminating the employee. But at that point, if you've been using the Adjust regularly, the termination is appropriate and is never a surprise to the employee."

"Wow, this sounds interesting. I want to try it out with Jessica. What are the four steps again?" I couldn't even begin to imagine a tool could do this, but Anne was three for three with the last tools, so I was eager to learn more. Anne pulled another reference card out of her briefcase and placed it on the table. I looked at the card Anne put on the table and said, "How does this work?"

Anne said, "Let's take an example from Jessica last night. You had said Jessica does lots of things wrong. When we use the Adjust, we select *one* specific, observable behavior we want to modify. This doesn't mean we can't address all of her undesired behaviors. However, when we use the Adjust, we address one specific behavior at a time. So, Emily, what specific, observable behavior do you want to role play with me to adjust or level-set one of Jessica's undesired behaviors?"

I thought about it for a minute to try to identify the one thing Jessica did that absolutely drove me nuts. While there were several, the most damaging thing causing the most issues with our customers was she sometimes forgets to write down customer orders. At Leo's, everyone, including the manager, is required to write down orders every time — nobody is singled out. This ensures a consistent customer experience. I had asked her before to write them down, and she told me she forgot. I didn't know what to say, so I just let it go. I told Anne, "She sometimes doesn't write down customer orders, and when she forgets, she makes lots of mistakes."

"Okay, great! I mean, not great that she makes mistakes, but this is a great opportunity to experiment with the Adjust. So, while you are learning, you will want to use the card with the language to address what is causing problems. You want to frame your language around what you see, what you hear, or what you believe to be true. In this case, you would literally say, '*Jessica, I see you did not write down the customers' orders at table one.*' At this point, you wouldn't go into the fact you've told her before to do it, and you wouldn't need to say anything else. You would be very specific about the actual observed undesired behavior you want to see change. It's important to not use the language of '*I feel… or I think…*' because I've found employees tend to argue more with managers' feelings or thoughts. Stick to '*I see, I hear, or I understand.*' We also try to avoid using language of absolutes, like you *always*, or you *never…* Those subtle words become quite powerful when using these tools."

Anne was deeply focused on the card and asked me what I thought step two should include. I thought for a while and said, "Ok, I have a bunch of things I can think of."

Anne started off the sentence by saying, "When you don't write down the customer orders…" Then Anne looked to me to take over from there. I completed her sentence by saying, "…you tend to forget specific requests and bring the incorrect meal. Cooks make meals that have to be thrown away. We have a policy at Leo's that everyone must write down orders to ensure a consistent customer experience."

I asked Anne how far I should go with what happens because I could feel myself getting more frustrated, and she said, "You must keep your cool. What is great is that you have an expectation, or policy, about this already in place. In this case, you wouldn't say, the consequences are 'you could be terminated'. We are not trying to change behavior using fear. This not what the Adjust is about. We are working to modify a specific behavior out of the employee's awareness and let them know what is expected of them. Does this make sense, Emily?"

"Yeah, so with Jessica, my goal is for her to know we have a policy about writing down customer orders. We also have one for getting customers their drinks in less than two minutes. When she doesn't follow the standards we have in place, things happen impacting everyone else. For example, the cooks make the wrong meal, and we have to throw out perfectly good food because a detail was missed. Is this what you mean?"

"Yes, Emily, that is exactly right! It doesn't have to be a laundry list. You share just enough to bring awareness of the ripple effect of her behavior." The Adjust is all about catching and fixing issues when they are small and at the time they happen...and before they have turned into willful insubordination. Willful insubordination is when an employee intentionally refuses to obey an employer's lawful and reasonable orders. Because you have a policy in place regarding this behavior, she has an opportunity to get back on track by your making her aware."

Anne focused our attention back on the card and pointed to number three. "For number three, this is where you give Jessica an opportunity to share *her* perspective by simply saying, *'Help me understand why you made that choice.'* Now, this is an important part of this tool. Write this down in your notes. *'Do not engage in defending or arguing with what she tells you. Just listen. Listen to exactly what she says, make a note of it in your head, but don't argue with it'*. You are not asking her why so you can shut her down. You're asking her why so she can be heard. Frontline workers are generally only told, not asked. This is a powerful part of the Adjust."

Anne went on about step three. "Jessica might say something you're not aware of. For example, she could say, *'We're out of order books."* In that case, it would be your responsibility to ensure we don't run out of order books. Or, she could say, *'I just don't want to.'* In any case, if the reason she provides is something within your power to accommodate, like ensuring we have enough order books in stock, it is an easy fix. If she doesn't because doesn't want to, you can manage through that as well.

"This is where step four comes in. For step four, you simply say, *'I hear what you're saying. Moving forward, I need you to write down the customers' orders. No exceptions. If we are out of order books, I would expect you to come tell me. What will you do the next time there is a scenario similar to this one?'* Does this make sense? You're putting the burden of responsibility to adjust their behavior back to the employee. The conversation should end with Jessica saying, *'I will write down the orders.'* Her verbal commitment to the expectation lays the groundwork for your Position to Notice. When you see her writing down the order, you can provide a 'Keep It Up'. Remember the ratio of three Keep It Ups to one Adjust? If you are keeping balanced feedback, you will have earned the right to address with the Adjust. It's not a 'tough' conversation when spotted during Position to Notice and balance with more Keep it Ups. Does that all make sense?"

"Whew, yes it does make sense. I'm a little nervous about using it today. Can we do another example together? Can I try it on you?" I felt like I understood the language and all, but I just wasn't sure of how it may play out when I was actually walking through the Adjust in real life. Anne agreed, so we picked another specific thing Jessica does causing customer problems on a nightly basis. She forgets to get drinks for the customers sometimes.

"Okay, Emily, imagine I'm Jessica. The problem is I forget to get drinks for customers sometimes. Before you jump into step one, think for a moment about whether the expectation has been established for all employees. If not, that has to be done before you can hold her accountable... even if no one else is having trouble with it. Has the expectation been set?"

"Yes, but only recently. Tim has just started rolling out policies for all of his locations. The Leo's off Bluebell Street runs like a machine, so he is working to make all of his restaurants be the same." It sort of dawned on me that these new rules were new, and it was up to me to ensure everyone was aware of and understood them.

Anne tapped on the table and said, "Also, write this in your notes. *'Managers should perform the Adjust in a private meeting and not with other employees present.'* This is important in the early days because you're working to build rapport and asking for their feedback. Now if the culture at Leo's was open to corrective feedback, you could let her know on the spot. That is the ideal we are working toward. Are you ready to try it out?"

I felt a little lump in my throat and hesitated a bit. It's so weird because I knew it wasn't real but it was about to become very real when Jessica came in. Anne reminded me we were just practicing. After this, we could do a few more so I felt comfortable. We both knew I was going to have to use this tool tonight, and I was a little nervous about it. Actually, I was a lot nervous about it because I've never really had to give feedback like this before. "Okay, here goes..." I looked at Anne and imagined her being Jessica.

"Hey Jessica, I need to speak with you for a minute. Can you come back to the office with me?"

Anne was acting the part and sort of shrugged her shoulders at me and said, "Sure."

I looked at the card for guidance and began. "Jessica, last night with the party of eight on table ten, I saw that you didn't write down their order. As a result, Milo had to remake the chicken parmesan because the customer had specifically requested the sauce be on the side. We have a policy that everyone has to write down the order – even me. Not writing down this order impacted the customer's experience, our kitchen, your tip, and might continue to impact us through a poor online review." I felt pretty nervous but also felt like I wasn't getting angry like I had expected.

Anne shrugged her shoulders again and said, "I didn't know it was like a policy that everyone has to do all the time."

"Fair enough," I said. "This is a newer policy that Tim rolled out. I apologize if I wasn't clear in letting everyone know that it is a requirement." I took a deep breath and continued, "I'll be sure to remind everyone in the Huddle tomorrow since we do have a few new policies to ensure customers have a consistent experience."

"Ok, "Anne replied. "I'm sorry."

I nodded my head in understanding and wasn't sure if I needed to go on. "Thank you for listening. Moving forward, just to be clear, everyone has to write down orders all the time. Next time, what choice will you make?"

Anne nodded her head affirming my first attempt at the Adjust. "I will write down the orders."

I felt pretty good about the practice with Anne. I needed to see the Adjust card while I was using it, though, and I told Anne I was worried that I'm might forget something.

Anne assured me to just hang the card on the wall in the back office with the other two cards and to casually refer to it until it came naturally to me. Anne told me she used this four-step approach on nearly a daily basis. She said she used it with her husband, her kids, her coworkers, and in time, it had become her go-to tool when someone was doing something needing to be adjusted. I thought it was a good idea and decided to practice it on my roommates, too.

Anne and I went through a few more scenarios, and each time Anne acted a little different so I could experience a variety of responses. Each time I did the Adjust, I got to experience that it doesn't have anything to do with having a "tough or difficult" conversation with someone. It made me understand that I can't hold someone accountable to an expectation that they were not aware of. That was huge for me. On the other hand, if I've been in a Position to Notice, then catching employees doing something right or needing a quick adjustment was just that. I felt ready for tonight and ready to address Jessica. Anne left for her conference, and I looked forward to letting her know how it went.

When the crew came in, I yelled, "Hey guys, Huddle time – come on up front!" Everyone came up, and one of the cook's said, "What the plan, coach?" I smiled, surprised at the reaction from the team. "Tonight, I want to try something a little different. I've been reading some of our online reviews, and I saw there were a number of them mentioning we weren't terribly friendly. 'Great food, decent service, but not terribly friendly.' So, let's do an experiment and be conscious of smiling and making eye contact with each customer tonight. It's Saturday night, and the conference down the road is still in full swing. Let's give it a whirl and see how it goes. Every customer: smile and eye contact. I'll try to remind everyone while I'm walking about, so don't take it personally if I prompt you to smile.

Sound like a plan?" Everyone nodded. "Ok, let's do it! Oh, and Jessica, I need to see you in the back for a minute."

Everyone started getting ready for the doors to open, and Jessica followed me to the back office. My heart started pounding a bit, and I could feel my hands getting a little clammy. I closed the door, and she sort of shocked me by saying, "Am I getting fired?"

I sort of shook my head and said, "No, you're not getting fired. However, I saw that didn't write down customer orders last night. I should have addressed it when I saw it, but nonetheless, we have a policy that everyone must write down customers every time – even me. When you don't write them down, it impacts everyone in the restaurant in ways you may not be aware of. Help me understand why you don't write them down." I felt like this was going pretty well so far, but step three was the moment of truth. How was she going to react? I felt ready for a number of responses since I'd played this out in my mind a bunch of times when I went to bed last night.

"I don't write them down because I'm too busy. I have too many tables, and it takes too long to write down every little detail." She was visibly upset. I listened to her and nodded in acknowledgement of what she was saying.

"I hear ya. This place is crazy busy, but the extra time being taken to fix your mistakes is more likely making your work even harder. Moving forward I need you to write them down. Every table. Every time. Tim is working hard to create a consistent customer experience at all of his Leo's locations, and this is one of the policies supporting that. There have been a few new ones, so I will remind everyone at our Huddle tomorrow to keep us on track. Moving forward, what will you do regarding orders?"

Jessica sort of smiled and said, "I will write them down."

"Fantastic!" I felt way calmer and matter of fact than I thought. She seemed to understand, and with momentum working in my favor, I opened the desk drawer and handed her a small server pad and a pencil and thanked her for her time and attention.

After Jessica left the office, I did a little victory dance and thought about writing the Adjust on my hand. Kidding, of course, this was by far the most valuable tool Anne had shared. The tools just kept getting better, and I couldn't wait to learn about tool five.

Anne came in for dinner at her usual time, and she must have seen how well it worked from the enormous smile on my face. She gave me a double thumbs up from across the restaurant, and I did it right back to her.

At our closing Huddle, I could feel things were changing just a little bit for the better each day. My employees were showing up a little earlier than normal, just a couple of minutes earlier, but in this business, it's a big deal. I let my team know to Keep it Up with their smiles and positive attitude. From what I could see, it looked well-received by the customers. I appreciated their playing along. It was a good night.

TOOL 5: The BLOCK or TACKLE

I have to admit, I was a little sad today would be my last day with Anne. I knew her conference was ending, and she would be heading back to Phoenix tomorrow. I couldn't believe how much I had learned in the past five days. With the changes I see in myself, I can see a distinct change in my employees as well. The four tools I've learned over the past four days were so easy to learn and a little challenging at times to do or work through. Using all of the tools daily has created powerful new conversations with my team I would have never anticipated.

As 11:00AM came, Anne popped in with her usual, happy smile. I got us both an iced tea and rubbed my hands together in anticipation of the fifth tool. "Hello, Anne! I'm so excited to learn about our fifth and final tool."

Anne laughed and said, "Well, this may be the fifth, but it's far from the final tool. There are many more to learn about, and as you grow, you'll find more tools to put in your tool belt. Some will be from me; some will be from books you read or people you've met; and some will be those you develop yourself. Consider this to be the first bricks on your path to becoming a great manager. It's a journey, and after twenty-five years in business and training people, I'm still discovering and creating new tools to help others. I suppose it's just part of my hard wiring, but I find great reward in seeing frontline managers, like you, develop and grow into great leaders."

"I can't thank you enough, Anne." I meant it. I couldn't express to her how much these tools had already made an impact in my life at Leo's and outside of work as well. I used the Adjust on my friend because she has a habit of saying she'll call and then forgets. It was amazing. When I got to the 'Help me understand why you don't call," she told me that she didn't realize that I was actually waiting for her to call. I had started resenting my friend because she wouldn't follow through. This all made me realize that I hadn't shared with my friend how it affected me, and as a result, she told me that she would work harder at following through but to tell her if she didn't. These tools were impacting my personal life as much as my work life. It was crazy.

"Okay, Anne, what is tool five called?" I eagerly awaited her response.

Anne pulled a card out of her briefcase that simply read *"Block orTackle"*.

"Block or Tackle? What the heck is Block or Tackle? Your cards remind me of a magician pulling lucky rabbits out of her hat." We both laughed really hard.

"Maybe I need to make a card with a lucky rabbit on it!" Anne laughed some more and then said, "Similar to the Keep It Up, the Block or Tackle is a tool to drive specific, desired behaviors in YOU, the manager. We all know that the greatest challenge you have as a frontline manager is knowing how to prioritize the litany of problems that arise during your shift. There is actually a third option, which is to 'Handoff', but we'll get to that in a moment.

"Based on our research, we know that the most common 'fires' that a frontline manager deals with are customer issues, employee issues, and inventory issues. Does that soundfamiliar?"

"O-M-G, Yes! Every day! There are so many things that come out of the blue that I have to deal with. Your research is right! If it's not a customer complaint, I'm dealing with someone not showing or being late, or damn inventory issues. I feel like the bane of my existence is putting out fires. I've often thought, 'I'm not a manager, I'm a flippin' firefighter!' So how does the Block or Tackle address that? Will it make the fires go away?" I laughed, but there was a bit of seriousness in my question.

Anne nodded her head and said, "I know, and yes, these issues are the bane of your existence; however, tool five will help you prioritize when to address what issue. But no, it won't make them go away. Let's walk through an example. Let's say the hostess calls out because she's sick. Currently, you stop whatever you were doing and you're filling in for her. Sometimes, these events are inevitable, and you have to *Tackle*, meaning you have to address right away in real time. Other times, the event might entail an angry customer on the phone, and you've been told by the hostess to get on the phone to resolve. In that case, it's not clear whether to *Block*, meaning delay your involvement until a dedicated time of the day to resolve or *Tackle,* immediately get on the phone and hear what the complaint is. Does that help?"

"Yes, it makes total sense. But, I don't have a dedicated time in the day that I can push things off to. Everything moves so fast." I liked the idea about this tool but still was not sure about how I would incorporate it at Leo's.

Anne took a quick sip of tea and said, "True! Frontline managers generally do not establish a fifteen to twenty minute block during their shift dedicated to resolving issues that could have been Blocked. They Tackle every issue at the time it happens. Do you know what happens after this goes on for any length of time?" Anne raised her eyebrows and looked at me.

"Yes, Anne! When I met you, my plan was to quit that night. I was exhausted and burned out with too many fires to put out and no fire extinguisher. It felt like most of what I was dealing with could have prevented altogether, but because I wasn't managing my environment, I had to react to everything when it happened." It dawned on me how these tools fit together. I realized that I spent far too much time like a dog chasing his tail. I mean, I just reacted to every, little thing I was told. I could clearly see that I wasn't managing anything, I was just creating more chaos. I was creating more chaos by not having a set of tools to help me decipher between what fires to address and which ones could smolder a bit before addressing.

"Anne, how do I know which ones to Block and which ones to Tackle...and you had mentioned something about a 'Handoff'?" I wanted this tool to work because I knew it would change everything for me. Anne pointed at the card, and we walked through it together.

"Emily, this is the most complex of the five tools. I will tell you, this tool only works when used in conjunction with the Huddle, the Position to Notice, the Keep It Up, and the Adjust. There are several steps to this tool, so let's spend a bit more time walking through the Block or Tackle." Anne adjusted her position in her chair and continued.

"The very first step is to think about your regular shift to determine a twenty-minute block where activities seem to slow down a little. Every business generally has some lulls during the day, so if you haven't already identified these, spend some time to notice when business seems to slow a bit. Once you have identified some regular lulls in the day, let your staff know that you will be in the back office for this specific twenty minute (or so) block each day. It should not ever go beyond thirty minutes off the floor. Does this make sense so far?"

"Yes, I'm trying to think of when that slower time might be," I replied.

She continued, "When the team knows you have a dedicated, set time blocked aside to address issues, and an issue is presented, really listen to what is being said. Most often, we sort of tune out after the first few words and don't *hear* what the actual problem is. Once you see or hear the issue, repeat it back to whoever shared with you. If you observed the issue yourself, take a moment to repeat to yourself what the actual issue is by categorizing it as a customer, employee, inventory, or 'other' issue. Unless the building is literally on fire, take five seconds to write it down (or capture the issue). If it's not clear, ask for more information if possible. For example, if a customer is upset and wants to speak with the manager, ask the employee if there are any additional details to help you resolve the issue. Are we still on the same page here?"

"Yes," I said, "Let me write those down... 1) customer, 2) employee, 3) inventory, and 4) other."

"The next step, Emily, is to ask yourself if you can Handoff the task to a team member. Just like in a football game, sometimes the quarterback hands the ball off to someone who can take the ball further down the field, and the handoff allows him to reduce the chances of his getting injured or tackled by the other team. Just as the quarterback is a valuable position and can't risk injury, the frontline manager is an equally valuable position and can't risk being taken out of *managing* the team. *Remember*, YOU are the most valuable resource on the floor. If it is a task that a team member is capable of addressing, by all means, hand it off! This allows you to remain in a Position to Notice which is essential to managing your team. Handing off will develop your delegating skills and gives the person you handed off to a sense of being valued and trusted. That goes a long way on the frontline!"

"Okay," I said, "That reminds me of the other night when the faucet broke in the ladies' restroom. If I had known of this tool, I would have known to hand that off to someone else immediately. Instead, I got totally overwhelmed thinking I had to do everything."

Anne clapped her hands like she was cheering me on. "That is a perfect example! Now, if you not able to hand a task off to someone else, ask yourself if the situation is urgent or important. The difference is this. *Urgent* tasks have an immediate deadline or a time frame associated to it. *Important* tasks do not have an immediate, hair's-on-fire timeline to resolve. The time factor is what determines whether it is urgent, meaning you TACKLE immediately, or if it is classified as important, where you BLOCK and do not address right then and there." Anne looked at me as if to see if this was making sense.

"Anne, I understand that urgent issues that have a time component and need to be TACKLED right away, but what do I do with the issues that I BLOCK?"

Anne smiled and nodded her head to affirm I understood how to use this tool, "Very good, Emily. The issues that you Block must be tabled for your specific, dedicated time each day that you deal with Blocked issues. This is the only time you should be in the back office resolving customer, employee, and/or inventory issues. If you (and the team) know that you have this dedicated time every day, it will start to become clearer to everyone whether the manager needs to Block or Tackle."

"What time of the day do I do this, Anne?" I tried to rifle through my day of when this might work, and I knew that we generally had a lull between 3:30-4:00pm. I wasn't sure if there was a specific time each day that she felt was best, or how to determine when to address Blocked issues.

Anne reaffirmed my understanding by saying, "Only you, as manager, can know when the best time to set aside to resolve Blocked issues might be. Some managers hold a regular, 20-minute block once per day, and other managers block two, separate 10-minute blocks with one in the morning hours and another in the afternoon. If you have a difficult time determining, you can reach out to me or to your boss, Tim. He may have some insights into when things slow down a bit at the various locations. If still not sure, be aware of when you seem to be not so busy each day, and test out that time as your Block."

She gave me another reference card to hang with the others. "I like this tool, Anne. I can see how this will help me at Leo's, and I might even use it at my house, too. Thank you." We both laughed.

"You're welcome, Emily."

"Anne, I can't thank you enough again for taking the time to work with me over the past five days and giving me my first management tool belt. I do feel a bit like a frontline superhero with my fancy tool belt." We both laughed. "I am going to test the 3:30 to 4:00 block today to resolve the issues that I Block. I'll hang the Block or Tackle card in the office with the others. Are there more cards and tools I can learn about?"

"Yes, there are lots of tools we use to coach managers at all levels of business, from executives to frontline supervisors. But, let's make a deal here. I know we went through these tools in a short period of time. You had a chance to role play with me briefly with most of them, and I want you to keep working through them. I'm going to give you some guidelines about learning these five tools before we move on to other management tools. Also, you know the quote about it taking a village to raise a child?"

"Yes, I've heard it before."

"Well, it also takes a village to grow a manager." Anne smiled, and I could see her passion for her work. "Emily, these tools become even more powerful when shared with your coworkers and other managers. When everyone in the business has a common language to use with each other, the results the company experiences are exponentially higher. Employee engagement is usually the first thing to significantly improve when these five tools are implemented on a company-wide level. Improved morale and retention are close second. So, the introduction to the tools is just the first step. When the time is right, and you are comfortable with the daily usage of the five tools, you can share with Tim and consider coaching your team – even other shift managers – on the simplicity and effectiveness of these tools. It would be important to share how they have changed you as a manager. I'm always here to help. This is the business I'm in. And, if or when it's appropriate, I can talk to Tim as well about how to move forward from here."

"That would be amazing, Anne!" I could see how things would be so different if all of Leo's Pizzeria's were using these tools.

"We also have an App…doesn't everybody have an app now…? Kidding aside, we developed an app to help managers stay on track using the five tools we've worked through over the past five days. While Leo's isn't ready for it just yet, know that what you've learned is part of a much bigger business solution. It's all good stuff!" Anne continued, "Until then, let's talk about the game plan, and then I'll need to get on my way back to Phoenix."

"Okay, what is our game plan, Anne?"

"Well, Emily, these are the things for you to work on for the next 60-90 days. We've done a lot of research that shows it takes 66 days, to be exact, to create a habit. Habits are defined as 'a settled or regular tendency or practice, especially one that is hard to give up'. Using your tool belt every day and using the tools in conjunction with each other will make this a regular part of your management practice. Also know at times, it will feel like the universe is conspiring against you while you are working to adopt these habits.

So, to ensure the highest probability of success, write this down in your notebook."

I pulled out my notebook and started writing:

1) Keep a daily journal handy to capture what's working and what isn't.

2) Start off each shift with a stand-up Huddle: 5-10 minutes to get your team on the same page for the shift.

3) Close your shift with a quick Huddle to capture what worked and what didn't.

4) During the shift, be in a Position to Notice to keep the team on track and offer Keep It Ups or Adjust to observe specific activities and behaviors throughout the day.

5) Use the Keep It Up to encourage more of the same specific, desired behaviors (recognition).

6) Use the Adjust to modify undesired behaviors to meet desired expectations (adjust behaviors).

7) Be sure to balance Keep It Ups and Adjusts. There should be 3 Keep It Ups for every 1 Adjusts per each employee.

8) If the Adjust is to correct a serious issue, follow up in writing with the employee or with a hard copy for their employee file.

9) Set aside about 20-minutes per day to resolve issues that I can Block, and Tackle Issues that require my immediate attention.

10) Be a Frontline H.E.R.O.!

a. **H**uddles – everyday!

b. **E**ngage in being in a Position to Notice for Keep it Ups and Adjusts!

c. **R**emember 3 Keep it Ups for every 1 Adjust.

d. **O**nly Tackle issues that have a deadline associated with them. Block the others to my dedicated Blocked time!

Noon was upon us, and I was sad to see Anne leave. I gave her a big hug and told her how grateful I was she'd happened upon Leo's Pizzeria when she did. Who knows what my path would have looked like if I'd had quit my job only to end up in the same situation at a different place. Without my new tool belt, I might have missed several opportunities to grow and develop as a leader. I knew I didn't want to be stuck as a frontline worker forever, but there weren't any resources to learn how to manage other frontline workers. Most of us get thrown into the proverbial fire called frontline management, and we usually end up leaving in the hopes of finding greener pastures elsewhere. Or worse, we get fired.

If we make it, it's generally because we're carrying the load of most of the employees and working ourselves to the bone, but not making enough to make it worthwhile. The life of a frontline worker or supervisor can be a difficult cycle to break into something better without any management tools. Knowing we're thought of as an expendable cost or a replaceable part doesn't exactly inspire the best in us managers.

However, I am committed to these five, easy tools in my superhero tool belt. For the first time, I feel like I can do this. I can actually manage the frontline workers around me and not just feel like I'm babysitting them. I can give meaningful feedback to my team to help them know what specific actions and behaviors can move us forward. I can adjust specific actions or behaviors needing attention in less than five minutes. I can get my team on the same page in less than ten minutes. I can ensure my team stays on track throughout our shift. And, best of all, I can now prioritize what issues I need to tackle and which ones I can block and resolve during my dedicated block time. I am tooled to spend the next 66 days moving my frontline forward and being a Frontline H.E.R.O.!

As Anne left Leo's Pizzeria, we waved goodbye through the windows. As much as I would miss seeing her every day, I felt confident that she was going to continue to be a positive influence in my life. I walked back to the office and was hanging the last of the five cards on the wall when I heard Tim, the owner, greeting the cooks. As I headed over to the kitchen, I couldn't wait to share my adventures over the past five days with him.

BE A H.E.R.O.

Be a Frontline H.E.R.O.!

- **H**uddles – everyday!

- **E**ngage in being in a Position to Notice for Keep it Ups and Adjusts!

- **R**emember 3 Keep it Ups for every 1 Adjust.

- **O**nly Tackle issues that have a deadline associated with them.

THE HUDDLE

The Huddle is a brief meeting with employees that creates a shared goal for the team to focus on.

The manager asks each employee the following questions:

1. What is one thing that you are proud of here at work?

2. Tell us something you want to improve today?

3. Are there any barriers that might stop you from accomplishing your goal?

The meeting ends with the manager sharing the action of the day, something the whole team should be focused on achieving.

AMPLIFY YOUR OUTCOME!

"A goal without a plan is just a wish."

~Antoine de Saint-Exupéry

THE POSITION to NOTICE

It's easy to get tied up with the work that needs to be done, but actively managing your team takes intentional effort. It must be prioritized.

To better manage your team:

1. Physically and consciously step back from the work at hand.

2. Ensure you are in a position to see and hear what happening with your team.

3. Look for specific behaviors to use the "Keep it Up".

4. Look for behaviors that need "The Adjust".

5. Be sure to balance 3 "Keep it Ups" for every 1 "Adjust".

Management happens through the practice of observation. Practice makes permanent!

AMPLIFY YOUR OUTCOME!

THE KEEP IT UP

People need to be told they are doing a good job, even if they are just doing the job they were hired for.

The Keep it Up is a great tool to encourage people to do more of the specific things that move the business forward.

AMPLIFY YOUR OUTCOME!

1. State the observed, desired behavior that is aligned with the company goals. Start with the words "I see..." "I hear..." or "I understand..."

2. State the impact of that desired behavior.

3. Thank the employee for doing that specific behavior.

4. Acknowledge your appreciation.

Reinforce the good, and the good gets gooder and gooder!

THE ADJUST

The purpose of The Adjust is to correct specific, undesirable behaviors and reset expectations.

1. State the specific, unwanted behavior is starting with the words, "I see..." "I hear..." or "I understand..." Be very specific in what you observed.

2. State the impact and consequences of the undesired behavior.

3. Ask the person to "Help me understand why you made that choice?"

4. Gain an "I will" by asking the question, "Moving forward, what will you do?"

5. Always strive to balance with 3 Keep-It-Ups for every 1 Adjust.

AMPLIFY YOUR OUTCOME!

People will not adjust what they are not aware of.

THE BLOCK or TACKLE

Every day dozens of ideas, problems, concerns or projects come your way. The Block or Tackle (or Handoff) is a simple tool that helps you determine what to handle now and what can wait.

1. Identify at least one 25-minute block of time each day you can work uninterrupted to handle daily issues.

2. When an issue arises ask yourself, "Can I handle this in my block?"

3. "Must I tackle this immediately?"

4. "Can I hand off this task to someone else?"

AMPLIFY YOUR OUTCOME!

Think like a quarterback.

From the Author

Congratulations on finishing the book! I realize it took a time commitment, and I applaud your perseverance. I hope your experience reading *Be a Frontline H.E.R.O.* has changed the way you see your role at your company and has shed light on a bright, future career in management. Like anything else worth pursuing, this is a journey. *Be a Frontline H.E.R.O.* is a great first step.

The next step is to start using the five tools with *your* team. Practice makes permanent, so experiment with one tool per week. Might I suggest doing a Huddle today! Recognize the first few times you use each tool, it might feel a little clunky or unnatural. Trust the more you practice with each tool, the more effective you will become at managing your team.

The impact of *Be a Frontline H.E.R.O.* can transform you as a manager *and* make your job more enjoyable. Your employees will likely see the change in you as you manage more effectively, and this will create a big impact for your customers' experience. Everybody wins!

Thank you again for reading this book. Be sure to share the tools with the people around you, particularly your manager!

~ Cyndi

www.GuidetoGreatness.com & LinkedIn.com/in/cyndilaurin

About the Author

Cyndi (Crother) Laurin, Ph.D. has 25+ years' experience in facilitating learning and organizational development. Her specialty is employee engagement and performance and operational initiatives, such as lean, six sigma, and Baldrige Performance Criteria.

She is also the bestselling author of *Catch! A Fishmonger's Guide to Greatness* (2005) which has sold over 80,000 copies; is translated in 17 languages, and was awarded the IPPY Book of 2005 in the Business/Career category. She also wrote, *The Rudolph Factor: Finding the Bright Lights That Drive Innovation in Your Business* (2009) detailing the phenomenal cultural transformation of Boeing's C-17 Program.

In addition to writing books, Cyndi is a sought after keynote speaker, general problem solver, and Certified LEGO® Serious Play Facilitator. She has a passion for helping individuals and organizations move toward their potential...and of course, wrangling Rudolphs along the way.

More information can be found at:
www.GuidetoGreatness.com
www.LinkedIn.com/in/CyndiLaurin
Twitter: @CyndiLaurin

Made in the USA
Las Vegas, NV
06 April 2025

20615950R00044